LOVE SONG WITH MOTOR VEHICLES

Love Song
with Motor Vehicles

Poems by
ALAN MICHAEL PARKER

✳

AMERICAN POETS CONTINUUM SERIES, NO. 76

BOA Editions, Ltd. ✳ Rochester, NY ✳ 2003

First Edition
03 04 05 06 7 6 5 4 3 2 1

Publications by BOA Editions, Ltd.—
a not-for-profit corporation under section 501 (c) (3)
of the United States Internal Revenue Code—
are made possible with the assistance of grants from
the Literature Program of the New York State Council on the Arts,
the Literature Program of the National Endowment for the Arts,
the Sonia Raiziss Giop Charitable Foundation,
the Lannan Foundation,
as well as from the Mary S. Mulligan Charitable Trust,
the County of Monroe, NY,
Ames-Amzalak Memorial Trust,
and The CIRE Foundation.

See page 96 for special individual acknowledgments.

Cover Design: Geri McCormick
Cover Art: "Road Signs," by Joe Morse, courtesy of the artist.
Interior Design and Typesetting: Richard Foerster
Manufacturing: Phoenix Color Corp
BOA Logo: Mirko

LIBRARY OF CONGRESS CATALOGING-IN-PUBLICATION DATA

Parker, Alan Michael, 1961–
    Love song with motor vehicles : poems / by Alan Michael Parker.
    p. cm. — (American poets continuum series ; no. 76)
    Includes bibliographical references.
    ISBN 1-929918-35-6 (alk. paper)
    I. Title. II. American poets continuum series ; v. 76.

PS3566.A674738 L6 2003
811'.54—dc21

                                                    2002038547

BOA Editions, Ltd.
Steven Huff, Publisher
H. Allen Spencer, Chair
A. Poulin, Jr., President & Founder (1976–1996)
260 East Avenue, Rochester, NY 14604
www.boaeditions.org

Contents

Whoosh — 9

I. THE WORK

Paradise — 13
Text — 15
The Island — 17
Driving Past My Exit — 21
The Cat — 23
The Piano — 25
Plutonium 57 — 27
The Librarian's Song — 30
Two Questions — 32
Books and Money — 34
The Work — 36

II. LOVE SONG WITH MOTOR VEHICLES

Television, Trees — 41
Pale Light — 43
Clear Cutting — 45
My Reed Flute, My Grass Sack — 47
On the Red-Eye — 50
Burn — 52
More Bees — 53
The Off-Season — 55
Salmon Seen from Above — 57
Before There Were Talkies — 59
T.V. — 60
The Screened Porch — 61
The Aquarium — 63
The Sibyl — 64
Love Song with Motor Vehicles — 66

III. THE PENATES

The God of Brooms Has Forsaken Brooms — 75
The God of the Bath Sojourns — 76
The God of Steel Wool — 78
The God of Pepper — 80
The God of the Vase — 82
The God of Wine — 84
The God of Draperies — 86

Wheel, O Wheel — 89

Notes — 90
Acknowledgments — 91
About the Author — 93
Colophon — 96

LOVE SONG WITH MOTOR VEHICLES

Whoosh

My friend, my love, my onliest affliction,
Why so sad? It's just one day.
And now, at last, come dusk—the light

Shredded in the valley o'er the battlefield—
We can climb the stairs to our amnesia,
Detonate the barbecue, and swirl inside

Our conversation built for two.
My dear, my favorite angina, now—
The moment, *now*—is but a splinter

Of our discontent, a jot, a mite.
Come. Hold my hand, and let us stop the shaking;
We are far from all our wanting.

My love, my ache, my doting critic,
Soon it will be night, and down below
The tents will each ignite in silhouette,

The mares will nod beneath their manes,
And the engines of war will drowse in their grease.
Come. From the balcony we can see

As the last of the day bursts into smoke,
Meat upon a spit, and rises:
Of the body, nothing more is made.

Come, my heart's-ease, my fracas and my thrill,
Let us fill the air with all we were, strike a match,
And *whoosh*, delight in our daily dying.

9

※

I. The Work

Paradise

On his sixteenth birthday he almost
bowled a perfect game, everybody watching,
Mom turning from her fries,
one hand mid-air.

Three pins standing.
When he missed he walked away
without stopping, out into the lot
where the rain had ended, raindrops

pearled on the hood of the Honda.
He was finally old enough.
In paradise, one of the greatest joys
will be sadness. A feeling

lining another, like a fleece lining.
Some blue inside a little pewter.
From the parking lot he watched
the clouds turn over

above a field of soy beans.
The beans were ready, this weekend
he would make some money,
and then he would drink a case of beer

with his friends, driving around.
He was sixteen, he was happy and sad,
which were somehow the same.
Walking out like that

was even better than bowling 297,
everyone yelling and clapping
and he didn't listen.
There was ketchup on Mom's fingers,

she was wiping her hand with a napkin,
her mouth slightly open.
The look on her face.
How people got out of his way.

In paradise, sadness will be free of nostalgia;
no one will need a past.
He put his foot on the bumper, lit a smoke.
Maybe he wouldn't go back.

※

Text

It has taken me forty years to admit
emotions have no words.
I express and repress, scrawl
vowels on a placemat,

test my artistry
against a poor drawing of the Acropolis.
Find me wanting.
Which is not to say that as a man

I am inarticulate by nature, or that the sunshine
moves through the sugar shaker
and then through me without stopping.
Or that even as someone who learns

in metaphor, I am much different from
the sparrow outside the Greek diner,
atop the crusted snow,
brainless with hunger.

On my walk back from town this morning,
I met a woman in her driveway,
one hand on a snowblower. Weeping.
The enormous trumpet of the red machine

blew the powder into the air,
noise going nowhere as she wept.
They seemed to me as one,
she and her machine, and what could I do—

the placemat folded in my pocket
sang itself a pretty lie.
What could I say? Sorry.
Then she realized I had stopped:

she smiled badly, wiped her nose,
and went back to tidying.
And I went back to trudging through
words, head down, humming out of tune.

✳

The Island

3 days, 6 meals, 8 coffees have I driven
just to see the island.
I have turned off the radio 90 times

to listen for the sea
whistling through my roof rack, Aeolian.
I have left you, speech, my tongue

dumb as a thumb.
I have taken off my boots,
one foot out the window,

one sock to the pedal,
yet another wild boy astronaut
breaking the law, flying

toward a hole in the bottom of the sea.
Yes, I have told the hostess, I am he.

*

I have been reading Wittgenstein:
"Since everything lies open to view
there is nothing to explain."

If only he were right, and the soul lay open . . .
Dusk falls, almost solid. As I slow
for an accident, the median streaked red and blue,

gashed, a dazed driver wrapped in a sweater
leans against an open door, dabs a bloody lip.
He looks my way.

Those were pearls, I think,
my soul laid open, useless, sad.
A woman in overalls waves traffic on again:

there is nothing to explain.
I am ready to see the island.

  *

Nature harbors no opinions;
it is we who think of *her*.
We make sentience

of her indifference, and we communicate
by engineering, adjectives, and awesome
violence. When I arrive

at the island, my soul
will harbor no opinions.
I'll stop my car

where *sea-air* and *sand-light*
become one perception,
all the world my affections, stitched together

by a muster of billboards, the dizzying gulls,
and a drawbridge open in prayer.

  *

Reading Wittgenstein in a barbecue joint:
"In what sense are my sensations private?"
I move the saltcellar, coffee creamer,

fork and spoon, check, checkmate.
I lose, I win: my bad teeth smile
at the pigs on the wall smiling

to their deaths, hunger chewing in me
a hole the shape of the island.
Somewhere, someone's singing—

amidst the restroom tiles,
someone makes of her voice an echo.
It is my voice, all echo.

Yes, I think, appetite
is private, and its cousin, shame.

＊

Tellins, volutes, clams, whelks,
sieved from the sea by the sand—
and aren't I the philosopher-king,

with R. Tucker Abbott's *Seashells*
hidden in my backpack, always at least
one book ahead of living.

Half-buried, eaten, a large
dead red fish
stares at the seagulls' invisible strings

with its vacant, planetary eye.
Why not? I think. Each emotion
orbits around experience,

the island a knot,
dark matter in my oyster heart.

＊

A dirty dog sleeps in the road.
His paws twitch: a running dream.
Off-season near the island

few dogs may be seen, as the world
of garbage rots in its juice, in its can.
I am trying to think through

history—is there an off-season?
Perhaps if the killing fields lay fallow . . .
but then I think of the soul

and its garbage, the purblind
rooting around we do
for meaning, food. Dogs, love.

At the drawbridge, in line,
cars have been found, idling, empty.

*

It is what I imagine.
On the beach, the boardwalk abandoned
for my own metaphysical Skee-Ball,

I raise a non-allegorical beer
to a sweaty soul, unquenched.
"A cry is not a description,"

writes Wittgenstein, and then he adds,
"But there are transitions."
Transitions, amen. Like a simple

glissando, taking off my shoes
and rolling up my cuffs—
and feeling the sand pour through my fist

like a word through its history,
to form a pyramid, an island.

*

Driving Past My Exit

Yes, my Captain, I was there.
I was the one punching the buttons of the radio

until the right commercial came on
and commerce was my friend.

I was happy as a full wallet.
No sir, acceptable losses

did not yet concern me,
and the unnatural colors of the clouds

were barely noticeable in the glare.
No sir, I could not claim to be

aware of horns blaring, or of
my heart

stopped at the light;
and when the signal changed and my blood

seemed to still, at ease, and the road
moved around me, and the foothills shone

like the store windows of home
lit by artillery fire,

I was not of two minds, even then.
Yes, my Captain, I contend

I acted alone. My lieutenants?
Of the fates of others I know not:

a soldier is what a soldier does.
And yet, yes my Captain, I admit

that war is unforgiving, and our advances
in night vision have shown us

what we feared. Yes, my Captain,
I gave myself

to singing, invested in the production
of goods, of prosperity jingling.

Yes, my Captain, I now believe
I was only following orders,

good weather and green lights for miles.
Yes, Captain, I was

happy as a new shirt,
and the music on the radio was for me.

The Cat

I have been trying to understand
whether this life is what we burnish for the next.
Or will we be undone.
Last week a feral kitten found me, and now,

mottled with ringworm,
she moans in quarantine in my kitchen
and hugs a catnip mouse made of felt.
A scrawny, contagious cat in a kennel—

she could be my heart.
Which is to say: *yowl, darkness, prison.*
Which is to say: *aria, nocturne, home.*
Which is to say: pushing words around,

the in-box and the out.
I named the cat Simone de Beauvoir.
Is that the name of my heart?
I don't even like cats,

which she pretends not to know.
What does my heart pretend not to know?
Working at love
means abandoning the burnishing.

When I first saw her almost dead in the street,
I sat down and waited.
She circled me, coming closer,
until I was stupid and put out my hand.

The two of us in the middle of the street.
How could she think I know anything,
sitting in the middle of a street?
Now near the end of her sentence

she scratches the plastic kennel to get out.
What could she know?
Which is to say: *need.*
Which is to say: *fear.*

So many poems about the next life.
To make the poem itself a moral act.
Which is to say: *heaven.*
Which is to say: *a larger room.*

✳

The Piano

Out the window of a brownstone
four stories overhead, a grand piano

dangles in a giant bra, strapped into mid-air.

Swearing at its swaying
happens in three languages;

a large bald man apparently in charge

giggles through his cough into a newly lit cigar.
He imagines that his crew might be

just fucking stupid enough

to catch the piano when it goes.
Perched in an open window, he straddles the casement

and follows the flight of a flock of pigeons,

those flying rats, every one
a note of music.

Someone loves him, someone new.

For four hours now, the piano has hung aloft,
straining, winched and stuck;

the head office has called in a crane

that has to come from Queens.
But before help arrives, oh how he

is tempted to climb out there,

shinny down a canvas strap
to stand atop that lacquered stage.

He would be on TV, and she would see.

*

Radiation seeps from the core.
Bees bop for the tulips, singing.
These could be two ways
I love you, or just death and life.
Two other ways might include

how sometimes around dusk,
say 5 o'clock, I find a way
to pull the ribbon
so that my heart unties.
Or sometimes I pull so hard,

pearls magically appear on my forehead,
but—*nothing, nope*—the knot won't give.
So I pull harder: I brace my left knee
against the back of the sofa,
wedge myself against the ottoman

(hey, there's a dime)
but the knot only tightens, strangling me;
and untying it would be as tricky
as convincing my mom
that she doesn't understand

who I grew up to be.
You understand me, don't you?
I croon to the picture on my computer
of Plutonium 57, the image of a knot
that constricts in streaming pixels.

You're my itsy-bitsy ootsie-tootsie.
And two other ways I love you
might include how I sing like a bee
when the tulips magically appear on my screen,
and how I disconnect my phone

to untangle the cord, dangle
the receiver in its receiver-less-ness
(God dangles me like that)
until 5 o'clock comes and it's time
to call you, now you'll answer.

I ready my question:
Did you paint well today?
But damn if I'm not stumbling,
tripping on my intentions
as though my shoes were tied together

by the ribbon you gave me
one night at a truck stop in New Jersey
approximately 48,352 half-lives ago;
and as you wound the ribbon around my finger
everything was radiant, nuclear

red and purple and sexual,
the light piling into our booth
from each minivan turning off the Turnpike.
But now I'm singing
into a perforated piece of plastic

that will transport my authentic words
through a fiber optic trunk line
to where I worry you won't hear me
over all that color
(the opera, the bees!)

in the avalanche
of tulips in your head
as you wash your hair in the shower.
One more way I love you?
The cursor beats: 5 o'clock.

Just death and life, and each instant—
even this, the moment
before the moment
the machine picks up—spins away
like a dime lost in the grass.

✳

The Librarian's Song

Her husband has run off with a jogger.
Looking for Updike? Check the computer.
She has called Main Branch, put in for a transfer.

Her husband has run off with a jogger,
a dancer, a waitress, somebody younger.
Looking for Updike, consider

the books about Rabbit, a prisoner
of America. Each year, twice a year
for five years she has put in for a transfer,

and obliged when asked to wait longer. No longer.
When Main Branch calls back, the librarian swears,
they better deliver.

Her husband has run off with a jogger,
she found out earlier, and the books on astronomers
have all disappeared, and her

boss wants her
to find out to where.
Looking for Updike, try Literature.

Looking for
a husband, try Joggers,
comma, Younger.

What is it with astronomers?
Each night her husband would stare
at the stars

as though he were there.
Maybe he thought he was Mr. Popper
from the children's book: see Children's Literature.

She's never sure any more.
If the astronomers
are gone, where

are the stars?
Her husband has run off with a jogger
whose breasts are firmer, younger,

a dancer and a waitress, a star
of a life not hers.
Looking for Updike, try Post-War.

When he called from the highway the librarian could hear
his voice and she thought he was dead, but they were
talking on the phone. The computer

was down, and the cars
in the background roared.
She could hear

the jogger giggle, titter.
That's what a young jogger would do, she'd titter.
And then when he told her

the librarian wept right there
at her desk, in front of two strangers,
a woman and her daughter. The astronomers,

the librarian cried, wherever
they are,
they're there.

※

Two Questions

The lunch shift finished, she leans against a dumpster,
catches her breath, smokes a cigarette.
The god arrives: What have you brought?

Only a brush, a book, and this, she says,
holding up the cigarettes and lighter.
What is important? She thinks the answer

must be the book, but it's not a very good book.
The book? But the god is no longer there.
She looks up. That's how a god should disappear,

she thinks. In a narrowing shaft
between tall buildings the light becomes shadows,
the dumpsters become monsters,

and the fire escapes drip with moss.
A few yards down the alley, a cat scratches
into a garbage bag, the plastic smacking, a sound

like applause. What is important?
Back inside the restaurant,
she checks the setups, restocks, tips the busboys.

If she speaks to anyone, she can't remember.
How like a god not to let me remember, she thinks.
At home there's still an hour before

picking up the kids from daycare.
On the table, the brush, the book, the cigarettes.
She'll need to get groceries for dinner;

she'll bring the kids to the store.
The brush, the book, the cigarettes:
something is important.

She considers how one of the objects
speaks to vanity, one to vice, one to learning,
although the book is not a very good one.

She flicks a bit of fluff across the table.
Of course, the questions might be symbolic,
since the god's a god: What have you brought?

She sips her tea, strong tea, China Black,
kicks off her work shoes, a relief.
What have you brought? What is important?

Good questions for a god to ask,
better than her own. She writes them down
on the back of a takeout menu,

rummages around, finds magnets in a drawer,
and sticks the menu to the fridge.
She checks her watch: time to get the kids.

✳

Books and Money

Because who has the money seems decided.
Because a one-legged woman in a housedress
leans her good hip against the stove
and makes soup from frozen vegetables

she doesn't recognize. Because she wonders where
her other leg was taken, how it became a myth
in the hands of a kid with a night job at the hospital
reading in the basement by the garbage chute,

hunched in the light of the incinerator.
Myth was a word she had learned in high school
in the story about the Greek guy who slept with his mom.
Her leg was a myth the kid could tell.

Because even on TV the winners
have been decided, and when they win
they spend all their money, and then
they're watching again like you or me.

Because a rich guy leaves millions to his son
as easily as vegetables make soup.
Because this morning she found a green garbage bag
full of books, and she laughed right there in the street,

thinking it was full of money.
Then she cried. The books
had no covers, someone had torn them off,
but no one would buy just covers,

that would be like living in the woods
and subscribing to *TV Guide*.
Because after the vegetables boil
the soup simmers, which is like

feeling something go
and then not feeling it again.
Because the bag of books was a myth
she would tell her group on Wednesday

when they got together at the middle school
to sit at the carved up desks in the library
and talk about what they were missing.
Because you can have plenty,

two good legs, soup, and money,
and still need to be there
early every Wednesday, to make sure
to get the desk by the window.

*

The Work

Which heart shall it be tonight,
the fist, or the little lettuce?

From a borrowed porch at dusk,
the light retreats in blurred arcs
across a well-angled lawn,
movement and stillness
indistinguishable, a kind of rhythm.

A squirrel hops toward its
death next door
under a deck and the perfect, watchful
wrath of Paco, the chiropractor's earnest mutt.

Or a heart as full as over-ripe fruit.
Or smooth and pink and inviolate
as a little rubber ball.

It was raining earlier, at the pier, too hard
to stroll amidst the tang of sea salt and fish rot,

among my dead.

A hatless Customs officer in a yellow slicker
had turned backwards into the horizontal rain—
ripped down the dock
as though torn from a page.

I had tried to notice,
to see everything in the one moment,
dry, through my windshield,

but I was left with the flat
slaps of the weather,
inconstant, indifferent to

the pig's knuckle heart,
the glass jar heart.

So now, later, instead: work.

(Is something missing preferable
to something unwanted?
Or does that count as two questions
when I have only been given one?)

There are voices inside:
dinner's on the kitchen table,
wine and chicken and bread and peas;

darkness slips
into the laughter,

a riptide.

The dog trots off with his kill.
The dog heart, the meat heart.

In the laundry room
all our heavy weather gear
puddles in a double sink.
Over there, away,

the storm cell barrels
up the coast, roll within roll
of nonbeing, all form,
exquisite and ordinary.

Yes, that's right.

The non-heart, the exquisite heart,
the ordinary heart.

※

II. Love Song with Motor Vehicles

Television, Trees

In my lap you doze, your breathing
shortened, slowly drifting deeper.

Will it snow? you seem to ask,
if words are also what a lover's body asks.

On TV the bombs explode,
too tinny in our tiny speaker;

out the window, woods and clouds,
the sky thinning, full.

Darling, what's that noise?
You grimace, rub your nose.

Such pageantry in cruelty,
while the snow begins unbidden.

*

Can smoke be hard?
The birch tree peels in curls

that look like smoke but aren't;
the bare soul consoles itself,

wrapped in facts, in fat.
Maybe every tree is

cloaked in smoke, expectant—
and maybe when I die I will become

what I have always been,
empty in the world.

*

A crow defines a bare elm,
the wind serrated.

Is heaven a place to come or go?
Heaven is smooth, says the snow.

Heaven is cold.
Beyond the meadow two birches

lean like lovers
propped up by each other.

In a different season they might seem
less festive, gaudy, gift-wrapped.

*

Hi, Mom, a soldier waves.
Snow shoulders every tree,

catches in the crotches, stays.
In my lap, my lover grumbles dreamfully,

a furnace kicking on unseen.
Tonight the news ends with the wind

rattling the upstairs, rising,
whistling, acute.

Bye, Mom. Don't be sad.
It's only television that we're on—

and the wind and the snow
are ours to sleep through,

the birches bending to an X,
fingers crossed, a promise.

*

Pale Light

A paleness to the light this morning
makes the meadow seem
both shimmering and dull.

Of the seven deer, one doesn't run.
Such politics, her suffering.

In a different kind
of tunelessness from mine,
the wind rings inside the wind,
the clear tinkling of cutlery,
someone's party in the trees.

This morning, there's enough
pale light and wind
to make me give up
all my meannesses, one more time.
Am I like the deer who runs?
It's fear. What editing am I.

From sleep I rub away the moon,
wander in the long, brown grass,
wet to my knees, to see
where the deer have been,
but find a government in ruins:

leaves pooling by the road
and a stand of birch gathering.

The deer's heart widens in her eye.
Why won't she run?

What a neck, all those wildnesses
straining in every pause.
Such senselessness.
What a gunshot am I.

※

Clear Cutting

Happiness, the eco-terrorists have chained themselves
to a yellow bulldozer in my heart, and in my heart
fir and aspen soar, articulate, diversify.

A Park Ranger stands guard, twirls a hat
upon a string, winds it up and then unwinds the thing—
and in my heart she is a former lover

leaning a hand on a warm hood, the engine ticking.
Behind a makeshift danger sign and barricade
the media clamor for a shot: someone knows

the Ranger's name, calls her name, yelling *hey* and *please*.
In my heart old growth is threatened by development:
the eco-terrorists link arms, their motley

uniforms a splash of tie-dye in the scene
against the yellow symbol of all crimes
I have committed, in which I once believed.

The trees are almost knowing,
watchful, willing; the flesh is able,
the former lover keeps

a whistle on a lanyard, just in case.
Even my son is there, in a clearing to one side,
growing younger, helpless, shrinking

in a sleepshirt, his bassinet, his little room.
And in my heart I'm walking around,
just another sonofagun looking for you,

in charge of the refreshments, souvenirs,
what everybody needs to have
from having been to the National Forest in my heart.

The Park Ranger whispers code into a radio,
unintelligible as always, broadcasts widely how
happiness has come at last, the eco-terrorists victorious,

and to all lovers, now they can go home
to loving whom they were loving
when they weren't in my heart, loving me.

*

My Reed Flute, My Grass Sack

Virtue never stands alone. It is bound to have neighbours.
—Confucius

In the cab of the U-Haul parked next door
an AM radio ruins "Ode to Joy."
The doors are flung wide;
the giant tongue of the truck ramp

spits out its welcome.
The doors are flung wide!
The neighbors are moving!

Forgive me, Tu Fu, for I am glad:
the wind comes and comes and is the same.
I love my reed flute and my grass sack
of indecipherable poems

plucked from the dirt. I love plums
and Cuban cigars and ice hockey.
Forgive me. I will not miss the neighbors.

                    *

Wait! That's my chair!
Those are my coffee stains on the seat,
the Scotchgard sucked to my lungs.
That is where I sit and write my poems!

I remember well the winter's day
the ice laid down its varnish
and the pecan tree rang, bejeweled.

I wheeled my chair to the porch,
as though wheeling my invalid future,
and I wrote a sad poem about the neighbors.
The poem was no good. No matter.

The chair on the porch was my poem.
They're taking my chair!
The neighbors are taking my chair!

                *

Tu Fu, what's a man to do?
I have stayed up to write
until the swallows scissored
above the muddy rhododendrons,

the gods slicing up the sky.
Even the moonlight knew better than I.
But now I am so tired, Tu Fu,

I cannot tell one neighbor from another.
Whose recycling is at the curb,
mine or theirs, whose laughter
constricts around my name?

Music jangles from a reed flute
and the sepulcher beckons,
the hot maw of the U-Haul.

                *

Exile. The neighbors
change the station,
writhe to rock 'n roll
amidst their worldliness on the lawn,

their coat tree and skis, a Weber grill,
and two large garbage cans
laden for Goodwill. The body

is an empty kayak in the grass.
The Emperor has been cruel,
poetry banished to the provinces
where we all must live

like dogs trembling in the thunder.
Where are the neighbors going?
Take me with you, neighbors!

*

It is known that you failed the Imperial exams,
Tu Fu, and so you were made to wander.
I gaze at the U-Haul.
Too soon the truck will clatter into gear,

and somewhere in the world another truce
between brothers will end.
In the kitchen I empty my grass sack,

words and brushstrokes, confetti
dumped on the old linoleum.
The Master said, "The man who
summons me must have a purpose."

What is the purpose, Tu Fu?
To whom am I a neighbor? Even
my sad poems do not say.

*

On the Red-Eye

Having boarded, having been
Strapped into our seats, tucked in,
We might all be children on a jet plane
Built of playhouse blocks, the pilot—

"Isn't that Sal Winston's boy?"—
Awestruck in a cockpit
Aglint with aluminum foil.
Already, up and down the aisle, early dreams unfurl. . . .

A tray table claps shut, final as a prayer:
    Let not the winde
    Example finde
To doe me more harme, then it purposeth.

Eyes closed, I see myself arriving
In my past—there I am, the smaller boy
Parading with his plastic wings
Among the dead in Mrs. Nikoledes' kitchen,

Something burning on the stove.
Now our flight is ready, a voice decides:
Flight attendants, please
Admit no suffering.

Next to me, too cool to be excited,
A teenage girl in black and black and platform shoes
Rewinds a tape, the muted whine
A sound I imagine she hears God make

When we die, taking back the given.
But then her tune begins again,
Memorized and sexual.
Taking off and climbing,

The ribboned runway left below, unscrolling,
Our plane banks into the smog.
I'm all, I know, memorized and sexual;
It's all that I've been given.

Thoughtlessly awake, my dulled animal brain
Aches with the pressure change,
But the teenage girl has fallen asleep
Somehow, a miracle, her music pounding—

She's aloft and falling slowly, until
Her cheek settles on my shoulder.
Give, take, give, take.
A stranger, I am steady in her breathing.

*

Burn

What I remember is not what happened,
not the pain from the burn but later,
the baths five times a day.
Troy burned too, I would say from the tub

where I read. And the temple.
My cousin came and sat with me.
Who knew she was a girl?
Of course, this was before my parents

were people, when they were just parents.
Before Kant arrived. Keats.
Sometimes childhood seems like
a path at night, the flashlight beam

bouncing all over the trees.
Why must the past be a metaphor?
How redundant, when every word
is already something else.

There were soft cookies.
What terror I felt
I saved in a specimen jar
for later, for you, now.

✳

More Bees

At dusk on my tractor, when I achieved
one-ness with my five-speed combustion engine,
I decided to grow up,

and so I gave away my childhood
to a bee. Oh, was he fat,
so gluey with pollen, nearly sagging

as he flew, every little memory of mine
now his, all my onomatopoeia.
Was he happy? As a bee.

But then I realized I didn't know
how to be a man
like the men in my neighborhood,

their ties flapping, speeding in the darkness.
Is it possible to drive a tractor
fast enough to catch a bee?

What hurry is my hurry?
On his patio in a different movie,
my neighbor on the left practices karate,

in one-ness with a barbecue,
meat burning with the lid closed,
smoke twisting to the stars.

Two backyards away, his neighbor
waves another giant spatula and fork,
conducts his sprinklers

like a big brass band.
The bees are sleepy,
their bodies heavy with our memories;

everywhere the earthworms
interpret, making more of less.
Just to step into the kitchen light

from all of that to all of this,
legs sticky, my tired arms tingling
by my side—in my perfectly

arcane knowledge
of how I have learned
to be at one

with a long dead Englishman's
idea of formal beauty, order—
is not enough, tonight.

The bees are humming in their sleep.
I am humming in my sleep,
this wakefulness, tonight.

*

The Off-Season

By the sea, sea oats have been planted;
on the sidewalk, a sandwich board warns the cars away.

As the breeze curls off the swells, always arriving,
the sea oats shudder in their suburbs, and a pelican

dives between the condos, a bird too odd to fly
or to have such power. Outside Saunders' Real Estate,

closed for lunch, be back soon,
a tanned man in a zipped windbreaker

warms himself with a cup of coffee and scans the ads.
Reflected in the glass the pelican rises,

and dips, and disappears.
One of us is here, the man thinks, or says aloud.

Beyond knowing, he is down to coupons, weekends,
a photographer who wonders what to shoot

instead of getting up each day in his dark room.
Somewhere over there he parked: down the two lanes

of advertising along the beach highway, the billboards
and the neon geometry like something washed ashore,

new and ruined, he has driven himself.
A man, a plan, a canal, he thinks.

In his biography opportunity settles,
sugar to the bottom of the cup.

A gull lets loose a cry, tawdry, wanting—
and then another, and then gulls

wheel into their cries, their hooked beaks
and illegible eyes, fifty gulls or more

circle the parking lot, birds from nowhere.
If his film were faster he would catch them all,

pin them to a bulletin board.
He can almost see the shot, the sunlight

permanent and emulsified, his future,
too many birds, and each pastel

squat building on stilts, shutters wide,
a shirt unbuttoned to the breeze.

✳

Salmon Seen from Above

Thirty, thirty-five, maybe forty feet down,
a small school of land-locked coho
flick and dart, six fish at play,

dull orange against the bottom-browns.
Their every act *becomes*,
pure expressiveness and wit,

for in runnels and rills they seem
to be delight incarnate.
And in the way that nature too often can,

they remind me of a myth:
Tiresias, reluctant, prophetic, blind to us.
But I would catch them, and I would

kill them and cook them and eat them,
and not only because I say so;
I would stay up late, drink wine,

read Cixous aloud, have silent sex,
then rise early to dangle a nightcrawler,
come and get it, breakfast.

Or my behavior might be better,
God knowable in all things,
but I would still catch them and kill them

and cook them and eat them,
and they would taste good,
God in all things.

The salmon congregate or not,
run together, to deeper water;
(is it merely opportunity

that turns appetite to greed?)
The wind is a form of reason,
and although I'm on the cliff above

and needed elsewhere, here I stand—
where I can no longer see the fish
unless one leaps.

Leap, damn you, leap!

✳

Before There Were Talkies

The heroine needs saving, shucks.
Vaguely Eastern European men in an isolated cabin
swear into their beards. In the valley

a prospector pans the riverbed,
his mule munching amid the sage.
From the plywood clouds of heaven

pour buckets of shiny paper rain.
A three-legged dog chews itself free
of a pot-bellied stove,

then skips away for help.

Afterwards, in the coffee shop next door,

one tea, one coffee, and a piece of pie.
I move a water glass, take your hand.
The caption in my head

says "Sadness" and then "Looks like weather."
The Wurlitzer in my head plays
three C-major chords, and then a G.

The silence between us is a question mark,
the sixteenth-notes of conversation, cutlery,
the sounds I make, thinking what to say.

✳

T.V.

Between storms, the sky collecting,
the cicadas and the tree frogs and the distant children hysterical;
the leaves of the sycamore fluttering,
violent and musical and incoherent;
not thinking, giving in to the elemental pitch and yaw,
the plummeting, the formlessness; when the sky finally

is almost but not quite overflowing;
and the clouds are a surface the color of a turned-off television,
flat and unforgiving, and somehow, yes, forgiving;
and from every cottage along the shore of the lake
people come, to open themselves like curtains parting,
gawking like newlyweds as she says, "It's t.v." and he says, "Uh-huh";

standing at the end of the rented dock,
holding hands, their picnic devoured.

米

The Screened Porch

Evening, the first wine.
Throughout the neighborhood, the door-to-door
salesmen stand to be collected, at their curbs,
smoking and laughing.

A bicycle rattles by; the lights
of the houses upon the hill arrive,
less than what they meant.
Like a stammer. Like what the day

has come to, finally, stammering.
Like me, here.
From her stake and lead in the grass
the dog pouts at us, sees

our porch begin to glow,
her people on television.
(Is that what she sees?)
Our porch is elevated, screened,

just far enough away
to miss the basketball players' moves,
their trash-talk in the park across the street,
to watch them from up here

until the night cracks open
upon them and their bodies, and the trees
fade into pure form, philosophy.
But first—thank god—

the ambulance arrives. And thank god
for one cell phone, and for how
after the rebound and the breakout pass,
when the man falls to his knees,

his right palm flattened on his chest,
and is puzzled,
the dirt and the sweat upon him
are as they were

when he was a boy.
What does he see?
The open faces of the salesmen
slide by in their van, as though

perfect ovals cut from paper,
lined up for him to count;
the van empties its van lungs.
And the screened porch

aglow across the street—
do we look on fire?
Like money burning, I think.
Like a television left on

well into the indifferent, precise future,
until what was becomes
an outline of what is,
something to wear, like a sweater,

as the night chills and the lights
stop flashing in the park,
and the day curls into itself—
a newspaper curled in its bag.

Tossed from a passing car.
Flying. Landing angled
on the bottom step
of a stranger's screened porch.

※

The Aquarium

What the boy likes about the aquarium
is imagining himself a fish.
A thought itself is like a fish, he will think

many years from now at the sea,
delivering his mother's eulogy and opening her urn.
The ocean's hair is a mess, he will discover

as he speaks about his mother's love
of gardening, and milkshakes, and the mourners chuckle.
Each word he speaks will be

a fish, pursued by his tongue, a fish.
It's fun to see the little motorized diver
float in the aquarium, and dive,

to watch the bubbles, and to imagine
gold doubloons strewn all over his room.
At his mother's funeral, wind,

the mourners huddled in a black bouquet.
Many years from now, he will be almost
perfectly happy, after love-making,

as he plays with his lover's hair
splayed on the bedspread,
his fingers like fish through the waves.

✳

The Sibyl

Steadying her hand, in fury,

she applies a baking soda salve
to her six-year-old's eleven stings,

each spot an eye, a hurricane upon his skin,

then stomps to the shed
and siphons off the mower's gasoline
to pour it down the hive.

Stand back, she says aloud. Good-bye.
She strikes a match. Good-bye.

The flame catches with a gasp
and a boom, and inside the blue flume
she can see what will be:

her son grown,
a sad lawyer in the Valley,
twin grandkids, two of everything,

and a gray spot on a hand
that should have been biopsied.

Whimpering on the new patio,
her little boy gives a little cheer—

and again in the fire
she can see him

nine, ten years from now,

pants down in the back of a clothing store
banging his hips
against some single mom he won't remember.

For this, she fries the bees:
for the tattoo he'll regret, the gin he'll steal,

the rummaging in her vanity
for loose change at 4 a.m.,
softly backlit in her bathroom
as she pretends to sleep.

For this he makes her kill,
for his perfect face.

The bees spill from the hive—

do they try to sting the air?

She stands at the entrance,
hands on her hips,
ready to swallow any who dare survive.

Love Song with Motor Vehicles

In their personal sweatshirts, grownups are humming and reading.
The day has arrived, swinging from the garbage truck—

soon the eggs will run
into the hash browns and bacon,
dogs will chase themselves to sleep,
and tens will lie with twenties in the purses of the paid.

I love you.
Let us wade through
the spills and slicks
to our bodies, rhymed.

By trains, the day arrives.
Grownups are pillaging the sofa for bus fare,
desperate, checking the clock, its crucifix.
In the flightpath, mixed emotions:
heartache, and something like happiness.

Do you love me?
When the fossil fuels are gone, we shall see.

        *

Simple math: 10¢ wings = 1 Happy Hour.
At the bar the early drinkers roost.
Whose wings are theirs?

If I could be the streetlamp on your corner
you could stumble safely
from your day
to the doorway of the kneeling bus.
(O let me be.)

The billboards would go by like clouds.

And then at home,
we would name our next dog Pavlov
and ring the bell that we call love.

*

A picnic in the woods, above a golf course:
beer in a can in a paper bag
but better cheese, and oranges,
and bread so fresh it tastes alive.
(You taste alive.)
Between two solitary, well-positioned Bradford pears
each duffer arrives like Rommel
standing in his vehicle, pointing.
They stop, they swing, they leave.

More beer? Love makes a game
of what other people play.

Across our towel tablecloth
we drink to the smells,
to the golf carts

whizzing over hillocks and down dales

like words through a conversation planned.

(In the gap
between the picture and the sound,
you take my hand.)

There are leaves in your hair:
I like them there.

*

Driving before the storm,
private houses sketched in, crosshatched.

A crow atop a telephone pole.

Blocks and subdivisions, the perpendicular, the sprawl.

In the late 19th century light
on a strip mall sign,
silver darkens to tin.

On the highways, the grownups
ride casino buses,
greet every tollbooth with a cheer.

On the side of each bus,
a vista of the Rocky Mountains,

a cloud for every window, a cloud to look through—

and more clouds
embroidered on a widow's lucky skirt.

(When the weather changes, so do I.)

68

                    *

I love you.
Will you meet me at the flower store
outside the station, underneath the awning
painted like a bower in bloom?
I'll be there come 6:15.

At the kitchen table, in T-shirts and housecoats,
the day folded and left on a seat on the train,
tomorrow's grownups
are humming, and rolling up their dimes.

Do you love me?
There are lilies on the median,
impossibly, too thin—

come with me to see them,

to shiver together
on the shoulder
in the waist-high weeds,

apart from ourselves

and from other people's lives
blowing by.

*

III. The Penates

Estragon: *All the dead voices.*

Vladimir: *They make a noise like wings.*

Estragon: *Like leaves.*

Vladimir: *Like sand.*

Estragon: *Like leaves.*

—Samuel Beckett, *Waiting for Godot*

The God of Brooms Has Forsaken Brooms

What are we to do?
It's not as though the weeping willow,

Seen through the little window
Above the sink, in the wrong light,

Captivated her, her dust
Swept into piles and then abandoned.

Or the wind. Or the long fingers
Of the magician, coins flashing.

No, she was like the rest of us,
At the table, shelling peas

Or reading distractedly, wedged
Between ticks of the clock,

Her soul gnawed to the quick:
She knew she was needed,

And if she trundled out the old bike
She had not been on for years,

Pumped up the tires,
And announced we had no milk,

She would not be back.
She was no different.

In the corner, her broom leaned
Into its body as all brooms do,

Long, light, elegant, fantastic,
And onerous and awful and beyond grace.

*

The God of the Bath Sojourns

Among the poor, his pockets inside-out,
One flip-flop in each hand,

His Hawaiian shirt misbuttoned,
The God of the Bath is believed

To wander *incognito*—
Mournful, tear-stained, taciturn

As a god who has
No form can be. There is

Absolution, such rumors say.
There is a heaven.

On market day, on the Piazza del Convivio,
A chair is set for him,

A new Chianti glistening
In a transparent plastic cup:

He is said
To drink it up.

And in The Terrible Times, every seven years,
When the floodwaters rise above

The laundry on the lines;
Or when the rivers bake to fossil beds;

Or when the sea parts
Like fingers untangling,

Finished with their prayer,
And the clouds hang their heads,

He is said to ask forgiveness
Of the Desert God, the Gods

Of Marathons and Sweat.
He is said to bow

Beneath his shame. And once,
Say the people of the South,

In such a season of avalanche and eruption,
He was thought to seek refuge

In a simple room among us.
There, they say, he locked the door,

Ran the water, lit a score of candles,
And took comfort all alone:

Two wooden ships, three rubber sharks,
Tiny, tiny in his mighty hands.

✳

The God of Steel Wool

They are insignificant, and she feels for them
(Her bushy ones, her nothings, her splattered mud),

For they dream the dreams of wanderers.
What is there?

They ask each other
In the darkness of each other.

What is wind?
(Her twisted ones, her spots of rot, her inside-outs.)

And never more than alone,
They molder on a bench,

A rag and a bottle for friends.
(Her sparrow eggs, her vowels, her little moons.)

The other gods?
O to have such jubilant indifference,

Neither a vision nor a presence be.
(Her clouds, her silly clouds.)

But this is not her fate.
The day begins, she does her chores,

Mops the floor, rinses out the mop,
Bleaches all the countertops.

She breakfasts: black coffee and a roll.
Then she dresses—first the leggings,

The iron mail, the lovely
Plumèd helmet with its hingèd cheeks—

And finally in the shiniest of boots,
She goes to garden in the rain.

＊

The God of Pepper

In her best gingham dress, teased hair
And Odalisque #3, the God of Pepper

Descends, makes an entrance
Down the stairs

Into the church basement, one
Slender ankle then

Another
Slender

Ankle.
Pot luck! And hers is the Ambrosia,

The gelid, the burden
Of each twilight spent

Staring at the cupboard's contents,
All those tiny jars, so different.

(Hers is a love
Explosive, every moment

In her gaze
A long night and a short day.)

But now she has arrived:
She stands behind the table,

The supper laid
Like a Bingo card,

And gestures with an open palm
At all the offerings.

She smiles, never speaks, poses
Like a sculpture—a god in the finest

Of traditions—only to leave
In a cloud of suspicion and temptation:

A string of black pearls,
Inscrutable and good.

*

The God of the Vase

Forgettable, nondescript,
Not round, not thin, not short, not elegant,

The God of the Vase
Seeks comfort in a crowd,

Visible, transparent, pushed around.
In the latest bar, you know the one,

The Marshall Plan, just off
The Place du Marzipan,

Where the patrons
Always dress in green?

There the God of the Vase
Can be found, though never seen.

But something missing is not
The same as something missed,

The God of the Vase insists
To anyone who listens, firmly

Lodged and anonymous
At a corner table set for two,

The lilacs and the honeysuckle
Exploding into scent:

Nostalgia is not desire.
And the God of the Vase should know,

The most religious of the gods,
Holy, holy, holy,

Half-here and half another place,
Half-full of grief, half-empty;

Snapping fingers at the waiter,
Never knowing what to order.

*

The God of Wine

Quo me, Bacche, rapis tui plenum?
Where will you carry me, Bacchus, filled with you?
—Horace

The body's a cheap hotel,
Paint peeling around the chandelier;

The screw-tops
Of the screw-top wines

Scatter in the stairwell,
Obtuse as augury.

The body's a cheap hotel:
Its resident transients

Come and go like money.
We are all a kind of money,

Spending ourselves.
The body's a cheap hotel:

In the hallway, an old idea
Falls to its knees, its stare fixed

Like the death stare of the poet.
(A Teutonic god kicks

The ice machine. No damn ice.)
The body's a cheap hotel:

In a cage in the lobby the night clerk
Studies for the bar

And the lamplight
Cracks open, bleeds into the rug.

The body's a cheap hotel,
Neither refuge nor redemption,

More than we can pay.
There is no darkness, only emptiness

On a stage set for faithless love
Where curtains open onto brick.

The body's a cheap hotel.
Into the lobby, spit from the doors,

Stumbles the muscle-bound God of Wine.
He straightens his T-shirt,

Then swallows his only line:
The body's a cheap hotel.

✳

The God of Draperies

When revelation comes, the God of Draperies
Cannot decide the difference

Between *in* and *out*.
A patio is *out* though *in* a yard, he thinks,

Nursing his ignorance
And a mostly gone Tom Collins,

The sunshine and the cicadas and the loveliness
Competing for his rage.

But a car is out? So what about a swizzle stick?
Out of the box but in the drink,

Then out of the drink and in the mouth.
A little bit in and out, he thinks, the vinyl slats

Of the ancient chaise lounge
Stuck to him

Like bacon to a slice of Wonder Bread.
And the soul is in? And heaven is out?

But when the soul is
Out, is it then

In heaven?
Time for another

Drink, a tall one, but only half.
Which is the way it is, he thinks,

With gods and worshippers and revelation;
No one is ever sure

Exactly who
Has been revealed to whom.

＊

****

Wheel, O Wheel

Ground to a powder by the wheel of the sun
I brush myself off: there are revolutions
to regret, bills to save like snapshots,

tasks to invent, to forget.
If I were the oak outside the living room
I would dream of birds, breeze, a flash of

orange just before the buses rumble, style.
If I were the floor I would dream of more:
the tide, the pull, the history of everything,

the sea alive with movement, somehow still.
If I were the wall I would picture myself
let loose in a field, aslant toward the trees,

one plate full. The house shrugs;
the moon snags on a telephone pole.
The clock collects me in its arms:

there are meetings to ruin, crimes to enjoy,
years to rewrite, too much what I am.
If I were the closet I would open in a dream

of fingers interwoven, water cupped to drink.
Out on the lawn the grass is tucked in;
the street runs to the corner

and stops, and turns, and runs.
Clouds shoulder each other across the sky.
There are cans to empty, resolutions to ignore,

a bird to shoo with a broom through the dining room.
If I were the hall I would go to the door
and step out, and be gone.

✳

Notes

"The Island": The quotations are from Ludwig Wittgenstein, *Philosophical Investigations* (Third Edition), translated by G.E.M. Anscombe (Prentice Hall, 1958).

"Plutonium 57": The isotope Plutonium 57 is a fiction; for information pertaining to radioactive isotopes, I am indebted to the physicist Dr. Wolfgang Christian.

"My Reed Flute, My Grass Sack": The quotations are from Confucius, *The Analects*, translated by D.C. Lau (Penguin Books, 1979).

"On the Red-Eye": The quotation is from John Donne, "A Valediction of weeping," *The Complete Poetry of John Donne* (Anchor Books, 1967).

Epigraph for "The Penates": The lines are from Samuel Beckett, *Waiting for Godot* (Grove Press, 1982).

"The Penates": These poems take as their inspiration the household gods of Aeneas.

"The God of Wine": The epigraph is from Horace, iii.25; the translation is by the classicist Dr. Jeanne O'Neill, to whom I am indebted. The poem was inspired by Fred Leebron's novel, *Out West*.

*

Acknowledgments

American Poetry Review: "Before There Were Talkies," "The Off-Season";

The Antioch Review: "Whoosh";

DoubleTake: "On the Red-Eye";

Electronic Poetry Review (*http://www.poetry.org*): "The God of the Bath Sojourns," "The God of Brooms Has Forsaken Brooms";

Field: "Books and Money";

Hotel Amerika: "The God of Draperies";

The Paris Review: "Driving Past My Exit," "The Island," "The Work";

Pleiades: "The Librarian's Song," "The Screened Porch";

The New Republic: "T.V.";

Smartish Pace: "The God of Steel Wool";

The Southern Review: "Salmon Seen from Above";

TriQuarterly: "The God of Pepper";

The Yale Review: "The God of Wine";

The Yalobusha Review: "Two Questions";

"More Bees" appeared in *Along the Lake*, Sean Thomas Dougherty, ed. (Ye Olde Font Shoppe, 2003).

"The God of Pepper" was reprinted in *The New Young American Poets*, Kevin Prufer, ed. (Southern Illinois University Press, 2000).

I am grateful to the Arts & Science Council of Mecklenburg County, the Seaside Institute, the MacDowell Colony, and Davidson College, for fellowships that enabled the writing of these poems. With gratitude as well to Tony Barnstone, Willis Barnstone, David Galef, Andrew Hudgins, Zoran Kuzmanovich, Jean Valentine, and Mark Willhardt, for their careful readings along the way—and especially, with thanks to both Aliki Barnstone and Thom Ward, for their zeal and insight.

"Text" is for Julia Reichert and Steven Bognar.
"The Piano" is for Susan Elderkin.

"Clear Cutting" is for Annie and Randy Ingram.
"The God of Wine" is for Fred Leebron.

And all, always, is for Felicia and Eli.

*

About the Author

Alan Michael Parker is the author of two books of poems, *Days Like Prose* and *The Vandals* (BOA Editions, 1999), co-editor of *The Routledge Anthology of Cross-Gendered Verse*, and Editor for North America of *Who's Who in 20ᵗʰ Century World Poetry*. His poems have appeared in *The American Poetry Review, DoubleTake, The New Republic, The New Yorker, The Paris Review,* and *The Yale Review,* among other magazines; his prose appears regularly in magazines including *The New Yorker.* The recipient of a Pushcart Prize, and fellowships from the Arts and Science Council, the MacDowell Colony, and the Seaside Institute, Alan Michael Parker teaches at Davidson College, where he is Director of Creative Writing, and at Queens University, where he is a Core Faculty member in the low-residency M.F.A. program. He lives in North Carolina with his wife, the painter Felicia van Bork, and their son, Eli.

✳

BOA Editions, Ltd.

AMERICAN POETS CONTINUUM SERIES

No. 1 *The Fuhrer Bunker: A Cycle of Poems in Progress*
W. D. Snodgrass

No. 2 *She*
M. L. Rosenthal

No. 3 *Living With Distance*
Ralph J. Mills, Jr.

No. 4 *Not Just Any Death*
Michael Waters

No. 5 *That Was Then: New and Selected Poems*
Isabella Gardner

No. 6 *Things That Happen Where There Aren't Any People*
William Stafford

No. 7 *The Bridge of Change: Poems 1974–1980*
John Logan

No. 8 *Signatures*
Joseph Stroud

No. 9 *People Live Here: Selected Poems 1949–1983*
Louis Simpson

No. 10 *Yin*
Carolyn Kizer

No. 11 *Duhamel: Ideas of Order in Little Canada*
Bill Tremblay

No. 12 *Seeing It Was So*
Anthony Piccione

No. 13 *Hyam Plutzik: The Collected Poems*

No. 14 *Good Woman: Poems and a Memoir 1969–1980*
Lucille Clifton

No. 15 *Next: New Poems*
Lucille Clifton

No. 16 *Roxa: Voices of the Culver Family*
William B. Patrick

No. 17 *John Logan: The Collected Poems*

No. 18 *Isabella Gardner: The Collected Poems*

No. 19 *The Sunken Lightship*
Peter Makuck

No. 20 *The City in Which I Love You*
Li-Young Lee

No. 21 *Quilting: Poems 1987–1990*
Lucille Clifton

No. 22 *John Logan: The Collected Fiction*

No. 23 *Shenandoah and Other Verse Plays*
Delmore Schwartz

No. 24 *Nobody Lives on Arthur Godfrey Boulevard*
Gerald Costanzo

No. 25 *The Book of Names: New and Selected Poems*
Barton Sutter

No. 26 *Each in His Season*
W. D. Snodgrass

No. 27 *Wordworks: Poems Selected and New*
Richard Kostelanetz

No. 28 *What We Carry*
Dorianne Laux

No. 29 *Red Suitcase*
Naomi Shihab Nye

No. 30 *Song*
Brigit Pegeen Kelly

No. 31 *The Fuehrer Bunker: The Complete Cycle*
W. D. Snodgrass

No. 32 *For the Kingdom*
Anthony Piccione

No. 33 *The Quicken Tree*
Bill Knott

No. 34 *These Upraised Hands*
William B. Patrick

No. 35 *Crazy Horse in Stillness*
William Heyen

No. 36 *Quick, Now, Always*
Mark Irwin

No. 37 *I Have Tasted the Apple*
Mary Crow

No. 38 *The Terrible Stories*
Lucille Clifton

No. 39 *The Heat of Arrivals*
Ray Gonzalez

No. 40 *Jimmy & Rita*
Kim Addonizio

No. 41 *Green Ash, Red Maple,
Black Gum*
Michael Waters

No. 42 *Against Distance*
Peter Makuck

No. 43 *The Night Path*
Laurie Kutchins

No. 44 *Radiography*
Bruce Bond

No. 45 *At My Ease: Uncollected Poems
of the Fifties and Sixties*
David Ignatow

No. 46 *Trillium*
Richard Foerster

No. 47 *Fuel*
Naomi Shihab Nye

No. 48 *Gratitude*
Sam Hamill

No. 49 *Diana, Charles, & the Queen*
William Heyen

No. 50 *Plus Shipping*
Bob Hicok

No. 51 *Cabato Sentora*
Ray Gonzalez

No. 52 *We Didn't Come Here for This*
William B. Patrick

No. 53 *The Vandals*
Alan Michael Parker

No. 54 *To Get Here*
Wendy Mnookin

No. 55 *Living Is What I Wanted: Last Poems*
David Ignatow

No. 56 *Dusty Angel*
Michael Blumenthal

No. 57 *The Tiger Iris*
Joan Swift

No. 58 *White City*
Mark Irwin

No. 59 *Laugh at the End of the World:
Collected Comic Poems 1969–1999*
Bill Knott

No. 60 *Blessing the Boats: New and
Selected Poems: 1988–2000*
Lucille Clifton

No. 61 *Tell Me*
Kim Addonizio

No. 62 *Smoke*
Dorianne Laux

No. 63 *Parthenopi: New and Selected Poems*
Michael Waters

No. 64 *Rancho Notorious*
Richard Garcia

No. 65 *Jam*
Joe-Anne McLaughlin

No. 66 *A. Poulin, Jr. Selected Poems*
Edited, with an Introduction
by Michael Waters

No. 67 *Small Gods of Grief*
Laure-Anne Bosselaar

No. 68 *Book of My Nights*
Li-Young Lee

No. 69 *Tulip Farms and Leper Colonies*
Charles Harper Webb

No. 70 *Double Going*
Richard Foerster

No. 71 *What He Took*
Wendy Mnookin

No. 72 *The Hawk Temple at Tierra
Grande*
Ray Gonzalez

No. 73 *Mules of Love*
Ellen Bass

No. 74 *The Guests at the Gate*
Anthony Piccione

No. 75 *Dumb Luck*
Sam Hamill

No. 76 *Love Song with motor Vehicles*
Alan Michael Parker

Colophon

Love Song with Motor Vehicles, Poems by Alan Michael Parker,
was set in Goudy with Hoefler Text ornaments, by Richard Foerster.
The cover was designed by Geri McCormick.
The cover art, "Road Signs," is by Joe Morse, courtesy of the artist.
Manufacturing was by Phoenix Color Corp.

Publication of this book was made possible, in part,
by the special support of the following people:

Nancy & Alan Cameros
Rome Celli
Peter & Suzanne Durant
Dr. Henry & Beverly French
Robert & Adele Gardner
Dane & Judy Gordon
Kip & Deb Hale
Robert & Willy Hursh
Archie & Pat Kutz
Jennifer & Craig Litt
Suzanne Owens
Boo Poulin
Deborah Ronnen
Andrea & Paul Rubery
Allen & Suzy Spencer
Pat & Michael Wilder

✳